For: Nayana Alexis.
From: Auntie Dawn
with love

To Yohance from Mum.
D.A.

WHAT WILL I BE?
TAMARIND BOOKS 9781870516815

Published in Great Britain by Tamarind Books,
a division of Random House Children's Books
A Random House Group Company

This edition published 2006
Reprinted 2008

3 5 7 9 10 8 6 4 2

Text copyright © Dawne Allette, 2006
Illustrations copyright © Paul Cemmick, 2006

The right of Dawne Allette and Paul Cemmick to be identified as the author and illustrator of this work has been asserted in accordance with the Copyright, Designs and Patents Act 1988.

All rights reserved. No part of this publication may be reproduced, stored in a retrieval system, or transmitted in any form or by any means, electronic, mechanical, photocopying, recording or otherwise, without the prior permission of the publishers.

Set in Stanley

TAMARIND BOOKS
61–63 Uxbridge Road, London, W5 5SA

www.tamarindbooks.co.uk
www.kidsatrandomhouse.co.uk

Addresses for companies within The Random House Group Limited can be found at: www.randomhouse.co.uk/offices.htm

THE RANDOM HOUSE GROUP Limited Reg. No. 954009

A CIP catalogue record for this book is available from the British Library.

Printed and bound in Singapore

What Will I Be?

Dawne Allette
illustrated by Paul Cemmick

I could be a sailor
And sail into port,

It is hard to work out
What to do with my life.
A doctor,

a dentist...

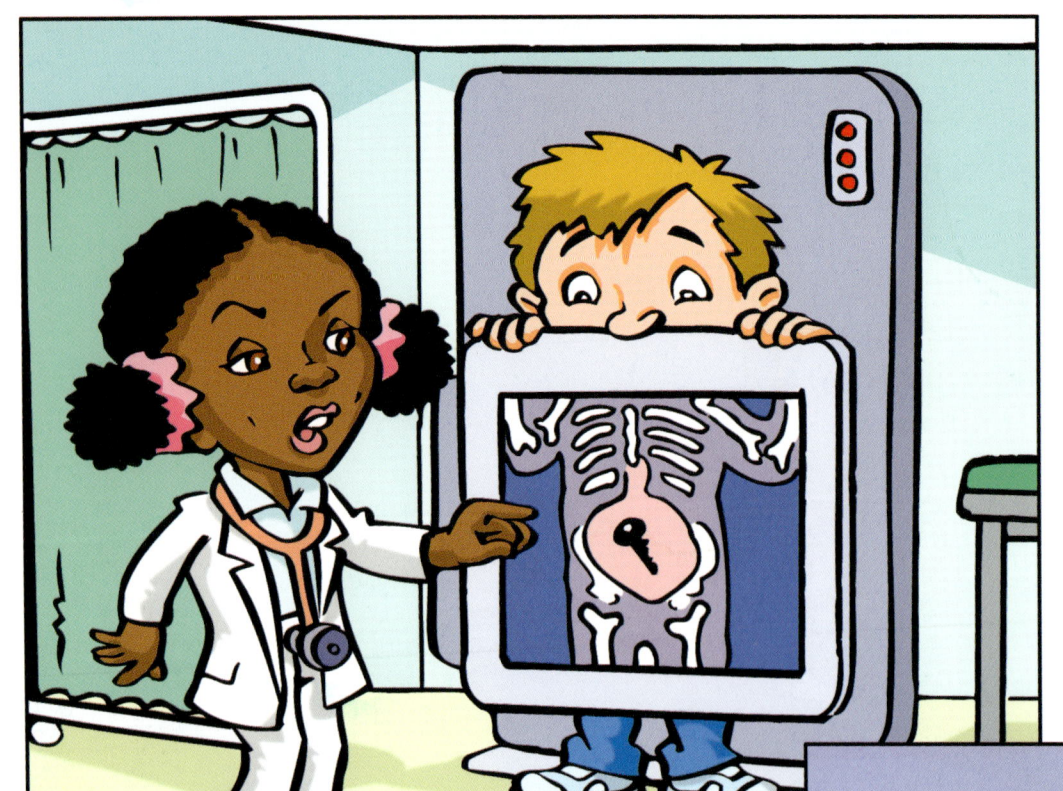

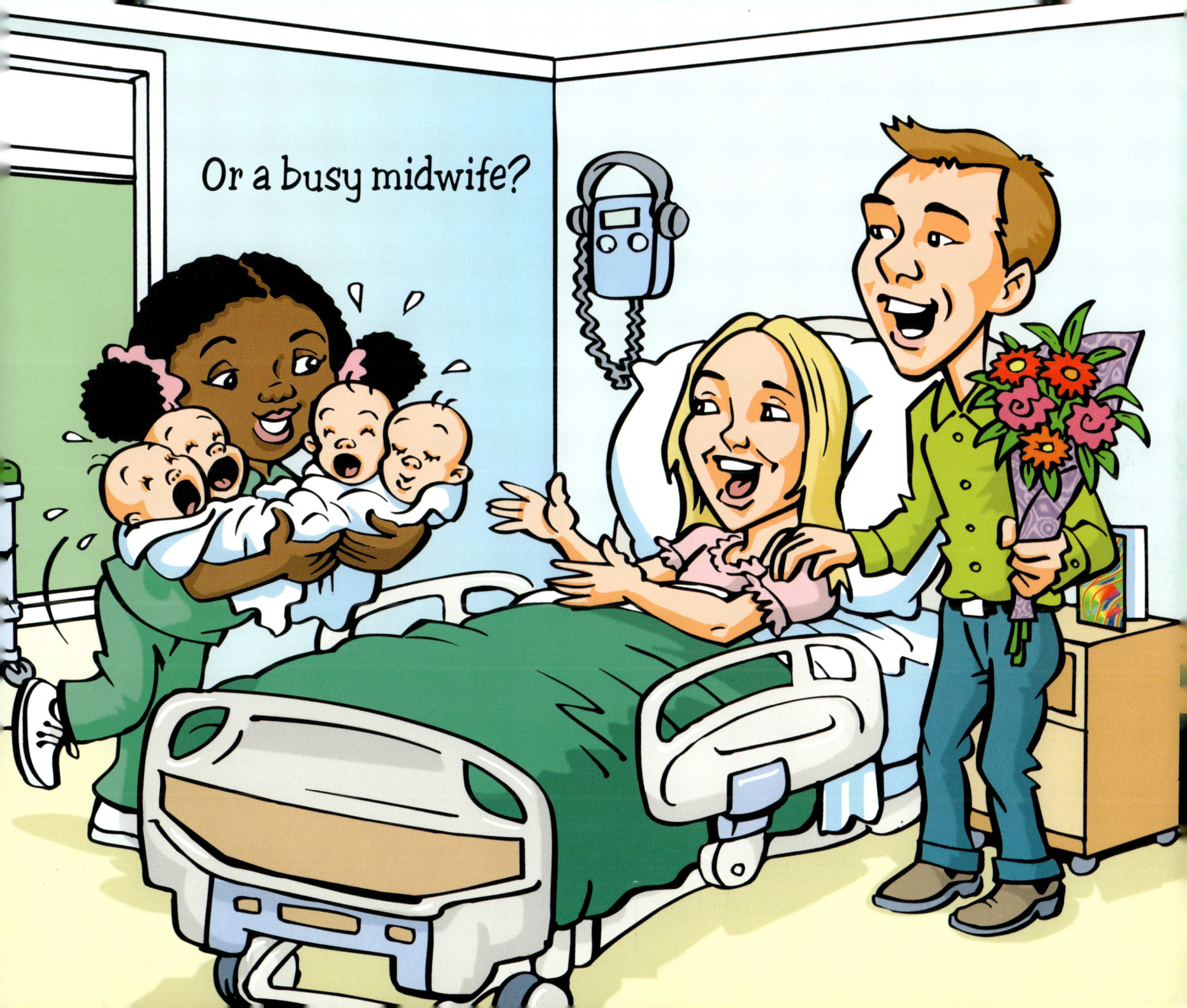

I could be a cartoonist
That would be funny,

Or maybe a banker
And take care of your money.

I will join the police,
If they let me wear pink.

A fearless firefighter
That is what I will be,
And rescue your cat
Stuck high in a tree.

I will work in a circus,
Flying high off the ground.

Or teach sign language
Without making a sound.

OTHER TAMARIND TITLES

FOR *What Will I Be?* READERS
Danny's Adventure Bus
Siddharth and Rinki
Choices, Choices
Big Eyes, Scary Voice
Caribbean Animals
South African Animals
All My Friends
A Safe Place
The Night the Lights Went Out
Time for Bed
Time to Get Up
Dave and the Tooth Fairy
Giant Hiccups

BOOKS FOR WHEN YOU GET A LITTLE OLDER…
Amina and the Shell
The Dragon Kite
Mum's Late
Marty Monster
The Bush
The Feather
Princess Katrina and the Hair Charmer
Boots for a Bridesmaid
Starlight
Yohance and the Dinosaurs

FOR BABIES
Baby Goes
Baby Noises
Baby Finds
Baby Plays

FOR TODDLERS
Let's Have Fun
Let's Go to Playgroup
Let's Feed the Ducks
Let's Go to Bed

And if you are interested in seeing the rest of our list, please visit our website:
www.tamarindbooks.co.uk